TOO COOL

Invincible
Iron Man

Phil Kettle
illustrated by Craig Smith

Black Hills

Distributed in
the United States of America
by Pacific Learning
P.O. Box 2723
Huntington Beach, CA
92647-0723

Website:
www.pacificlearning.com

Published by Black Hills
(an imprint of Toocool Rules
Pty Ltd)
PO Box 2073
Fitzroy MDC VIC 3065
Australia
61+3+9419-9406

First published in the United States by Black Hills in 2004.
American editorial by Pacific Learning in 2004.
Text copyright © Phillip Kettle, 2002.
Illustration copyright © Toocool Rules Pty Limited, 2002.

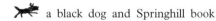 a black dog and Springhill book

Printed in China through Colorcraft Ltd, Hong Kong

ISBN 1 920924 11 6
PL-6214

10 9 8 7 6 5 4 3 2 1   08 07 06 05 04

Contents

Roberto

Marcy

Scott

Toocool

Chapter 1
Shark Attack!

I blew the air from my lungs. I could feel myself sinking down to the bottom. I wondered how long I could hold my breath.

I opened my eyes. The light above the water was all I could see. I started kicking.

I was trying to reach the surface. The light was getting dim. A huge shadow was blocking the sun.

Was it some horrible shark from the depths of the ocean?

My head broke the surface. I took a big gulp of air.

My eyes began to focus. I looked at the giant shark.

It spoke.

"Toocool! Will you stop kicking water out of the bathtub? Look at the mess you made on the floor!" snapped Mom.

It was only a little while until the iron-man contest. The bathtub was a great place for extra training.

I thought Mom would be happy to see me training so hard. The iron-man trophy was amazing. She would love to have it on top of the mantel.

4

Besides, I always cleaned up after myself—when I remembered.

Chapter 2
The Secret

Roberto and I kept our iron-man training a secret. We wanted to be the only ones in the contest. Why waste everyone's time? We were the only water whiz kids.

The real competition was between us.

We trained in secret. We also learned how to do cannonballs from the high dive.

Roberto said cannonball jumping was going to become an Olympic sport soon.

We also practiced diving.

We were on the regular diving board. It's a lot higher than it looks. I walked out to the end. I stood on tiptoe. I pointed my arms out in front of me.

I was about to do a double flip, and finish with a full body twist.

Suddenly, a voice broke my concentration.

"Come on, Toocool! If you don't jump soon, the pool will dry up."

I looked down. It was Marcy. She was sitting on the edge of the pool. She was still in her clothes.

I decided to skip the fancy dive. Instead, I did the biggest cannonball I could.

Splash!

The water went all over Marcy. Roberto and I could not stop laughing.

Then Marcy said, "You two are going to get it in the iron-man contest!"

We stopped laughing.

How did she know about the contest?

"See you tomorrow. Don't forget your water wings!" she yelled.

Rats! There was more competition than we thought.

Chapter 3
The Rules

The morning of the contest, we read the rules carefully.

We had to swim two lengths of the pool, race around the park next door, then grab our boogie boards and paddle two more lengths.

I looked at the trophy. It was a huge silver cup. It stood at the back of the snack bar with the candy.

"You're mine," I whispered.

I could see myself in the side of the cup. I was shocked. I looked really tough.

Toocool—Man of Iron.

We lined up.

There were kids everywhere! We had to get numbers written on our arms. I asked for number one. It was already taken. That was strange.

I was number eight.

I had one last swig of my energy drink. Mom had made it for me. She said lemonade always got me going.

Roberto looked nervous. He was jumping up and down. Marcy and Scott were running in place.

Everyone else looked scared.

I waved to Mom and Dad. I was feeling cool. I was a natural iron man.

The whistle blew. We were called to our starting blocks.

That lemonade must have been too powerful. I felt a little sick.

Chapter 4
Chasing Roberto

"**O**n your marks. Get set. Go!"

I hit the water like a torpedo. I sped ahead. I didn't need to look around. I knew I was in the lead.

The end of the first lap was in sight.

It was time to see where the other swimmers were.

I was stunned. Most of them were beside me and one of them was ahead of me.

It was Roberto!

I started my flip turn. Even under the water, I could hear the crowd yelling, "Go, Toocool!"

The pressure was on. I had to swim even faster this lap.

Two more strokes and I was there. I was in the wrong lane, but it didn't matter.

I leaped out of the pool.

Roberto was already running. He needed a head start. He is not a good runner.

Marcy ran up beside me.

"Move it, Toocool, or I'll flatten you like a pancake!"

Scott was on my other side. His eyes were popping out. His face was red.

"Watch me win!" he yelled.

I ignored both of them and ran even faster.

We headed for the park.

Roberto was still in the lead. I took off after him. My legs were like running machines.

Mom handed me a drink as I sped by. I took a gulp and kept running. I was catching up to Roberto.

Chapter 5
Looking Back

We raced back to the pool. We were in a huge pack.

I hoped a plane was flying over us. We would have looked great from the air.

I broke free from the pack. I was first through the gates.

We all grabbed our
boogie boards.

Roberto and I hit the water
at the same time. We were side
by side all the way to the end
of the first lap.

The crowd was going wild.

I threw myself into a flip
turn. I got back on my board.
I paddled as hard as I could.

I could feel myself pulling
ahead. I knew I had left
Roberto in my dust.

That's when I turned
around to take a look.

Something was wrong.
Roberto was still at the end.
He was holding his nose. His
boogie board was floating in
my lane.

Roberto was in trouble!
I had to go back.

"What's wrong?" I asked Roberto.

"I hit the edge!" honked Roberto.

I checked his nose. There was no blood. Then I grabbed his board and threw it to him.

"Keep going!" he yelled. "I'll be all right!"

I took off. I had lost ground, but I knew I could do it!

I pushed my body as hard as I could. My chest and arms hurt. I was strong, though. I could overcome the pain.

I was made of iron.

I had won!

The crowd went crazy.

They said I was an iron man and a gentleman—whatever that means.

I wonder if iron men are good soccer players?

The End!

Toocool's
Iron-Man Glossary

Boogie board—A small lightweight surfboard that you usually ride lying down.

Cannonball—A jump into water with your knees held to your chest. A cannonball makes a huge splash.

Torpedo—A bullet-shaped missile that is fired from a submarine or torpedo boat.

Water wings—Blow-up bags that little kids wear around their arms when they are learning how to swim.

Toocool's Map
The Iron-Man Course

The Very
Big Park
(Scene of Many Other
Toocool Triumphs)

31

Toocool's Quick Summary
Iron-Man Contests

There are different kinds of iron-man contests, but most of them are triathlons.

Triathlons involve three sports. These are usually swimming, bike riding, and running.

The hardest thing about a triathlon is that the events are one right after the other. This means the competitors must know how to pace themselves.

They have to have incredible endurance so they can keep going and going and going.

The most famous iron-man contest is held every year in Hawaii. This triathlon includes a 2.4-mile (3.8-kilometer) swim, a 112-mile (179-kilometer) bike ride, and a 26.2-mile (41-kilometer) marathon.

Most iron-man competitors are happy just to finish the race!

The Pool

The Not-So-Low Dive

The Splash Zone

6 7 8

Q & A with Toocool
He Answers His Own Questions

🏆 **Do you have to be in good shape to be an iron man?**

Are you kidding? You have to be in better shape than any other athlete. Even I have to train hard for iron-man contests. My natural talent helps a lot, but I still have to train. I have to eat right and stay focused.

Which iron-man event do you like the best?

I'm an incredible runner. My legs are like running machines. When all the other runners have given up, my legs just keep going. Of course, I'm outstanding in the water, too.

Where is the best place to train?

For running, I train in the park. I take Dog with me. He makes me run fast. I also train at the pool and in the bathtub. The pool is a great place to train for swimming and paddling on my boogie board. The bathtub is a good place to sit and dream about the big race.

🏆 **Who do you think is the best iron man?**

I think that I am the best at iron-man contests, except I am shy. I don't talk about my talent much.

There are other kids in my neighborhood who want to be iron men. Roberto could be good if he trained as hard as I do. I'm not sure if Marcy is an iron man or an iron woman, but I know she would be better if she listened to my advice. Scott tries hard, but he always needs my help.

🏆 **Are all iron-man contests held at pools and parks?**

In my neighborhood they are. They can be in other places—like near a lake or an ocean.

Are boogie boards used in all iron-man contests?

I'm not really sure. I think boogie boards are only in the most important iron-man contests, but you would have to double-check that. It is extremely hard to kick a boogie board for two laps after you've just run around the park. It's a test of endurance and strength. Only legends survive a test like that.

Iron-Man Quiz
How Much Do You Know about Iron-Man Contests?

Q1 What is freestyle?

A. A kind of swimming stroke.

B. Swimming at the pool for free.

C. Underwater ballet.

Q2 How many events are there in a triathlon?

A. Six. *B.* Three. *C.* Ten.

Q3 What is a boogie board?

A. A scary piece of wood.

B. Something in your nose.

C. A small foam surfboard you can paddle on.

Q4 What is backstroke?

A. A swimming stroke you do lying on your back.

B. Swimming in the wrong direction.

C. Scratching your dog's back.

 Q5 Should you eat before swimming?

A. Only if you're hungry.

B. Only if it's cake.

C. It's probably not a good idea.

 Q6 If an iron man swims four laps in a fifty-yard pool, how far has he or she swum?

A. One hundred yards.

B. Two hundred yards.

C. Fifty yards.

Q7 What is a cannonball?

A. A good way to splash friends.

B. A big ball that shoots from a cannon.

C. A special jump with knees up.

D. All of the above.

Q8 Do iron men rust?

A. Only if they forget to dry off.

B. Only when they get old.

C. Never!

Q9 Who or what is an invincible iron man?

A. A man who does the ironing.

B. A new kind of action toy.

C. Toocool.

Q10 What would you do if you had to compete against Toocool in an iron-man contest?

A. Stay in bed.

B. Start the race a day before Toocool.

C. Hope you could learn something from the master.

ANSWERS

1 A. *2* B. *3* C.

4 A. *5* C. *6* B.

7 D. *8* C. *9* C.

10 C.

If you got ten questions right, you're made of iron. If you got more than five right, you're made of tin. If you got fewer than five right, you're made of paper.

Soccer Superstar

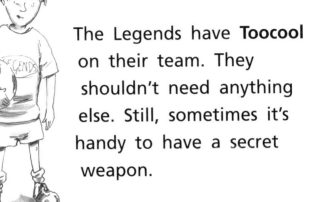

The Legends have **Toocool** on their team. They shouldn't need anything else. Still, sometimes it's handy to have a secret weapon.

Titles in the Toocool series